It IS Your Attitude

Luis G. Lobo

James &
Brookfield
J&B
Publishers

It *IS* Your Attitude

Managing Editor: Gayle Smart
Editor: Kay duPont
Proofing Editor: Rose Taylor
Book Designer: Paula Chance
Copyright ©2004

For more information, contact:
James & Brookfield Publishers
P.O. Box 768024
Roswell, GA 30076

Library of Congress 2004109504

ISNBN: 0-9749191-1-X

10 9 8 7 7 6 5 4 3 2 1
Printed in the United States of America

Dedication

This book began as a letter to my children on what their father believes is important in life. It is to Thomas, Andres and Felicia that I dedicate this work, which I hope they will pass on to my future grandchildren.

Thank you, Debbie, for being my loving wife and trusted partner these last 16 years. The BEST is yet to come!

The following message was inside a birthday card, originally written in Spanish, and dated October 24, 1975, which I received from my grandfather, Andres Arce, when I was 15.

Dear Luis,

Your grandparents, Felicia and Andres, are wishing you a world filled with happiness on this your birthday. May God provide throughout your life good fortune, health and happiness in the unity of your brothers and parents. On each day that passes, may He ***proportion to you a greater understanding***, so that you may find advancement in this world filled with toil but also with hours and days of happiness. Receive today from your grandparents a hug filled with love that we send to you from this land that witnessed your birth.

Andres

Acknowledgments

I thank my family for allowing me the freedom to dedicate the time required to compose this work. There is always a price to pay for whatever we seek to accomplish. I know they are pleased with the conclusion of the book, especially because they will no longer have to listen to passages here and there.

Thanks to Nancy Irby, Miriam Collins and John Lough for proofing the book and gaining copyright, since most of this has been a new experience for me.

My appreciation goes to Nido Qubein for his guidance.

A big thank you to Kelly King for authoring the foreword and always giving me encouragement.

Thank you, Karen Melvin, for your friendship and open mind, even though God called you home (much too early) before you could see the finished product.

I sincerely thank my extended family in Costa Rica, my grandparents and aunts who gave me a foundation of values that has served my generation well, my mother Marta and my late father Gerardo, who walked their talk and never wavered in their devotion to their children.

A special thanks to my professional family at BB&T. Without them, the path might have been vastly different.

Luis G. Lobo y Arce

Table of Contents

Foreword

by Kelly S. King

Leadership is about creating an environment in which followers are motivated by having significant needs met when they accomplish the results sought by the leader. Leaders create broad visions for organizations and provide guidance in the development of strategies and tactics. Followers, on the other hand, get the job done. Why? Because they **want** to. They don't act because they are made to do so; they act because they get something in return. Successful leaders understand that followers are motivated by whatever helps to meet their need for physical well-being, security, social interaction, self-esteem and self-actualization.

However, because of their own beliefs, equally motivated people can act very differently in similar circumstances based on their beliefs. When a someone's behavior is inconsistent with his or her beliefs, the result is cognitive dissonance, which causes the person to seek balance. In searching for balance, he or she tends to change beliefs or behaviors. Therefore, effective leaders should change the beliefs of their followers so they are aligned with the desired behavior. In other words, teach your followers why you want them to act in a certain way. Leaders are teachers! In addition to changing beliefs, leaders should provide positive, motivational reinforcement.

While many specific beliefs influence a person's behavior in most situations, we usually have one overriding belief that impacts much of our success in life. We have to make a choice about how we will view life in general—positively or negatively. Choosing a positive attitude will affect how happy we are and how successful we will be. Most of us have God-given advantages in life, such as the ability to walk, talk, hear and see, and most of us wouldn't give up even **one** of our advantages to eliminate our problems. Consequently, we should be positive about the simple, basic, most important aspects of life and realize how blessed we are. Actually, we should be outright enthusiastic about it! People, especially leaders, who go about life with an enthusiastic and positive attitude are effective because the people they lead appreciate their enthusiasm. It helps them be happier and more successful themselves.

Leaders also accept personal accountability or responsibility, as well as themselves and their actions. Successful people adapt the philosophy, "If it is to be, it is up to me," which is a statement of commitment to do the best we can with what we have and not blame someone or something else. Combining an enthusiastic, positive attitude with a strong sense of personal ownership makes life meaningful, successful and enjoyable. Having the responsibility to lead others is a wonderful opportunity that should be executed with a commitment to help your team be the best it can be while enjoying the path to success!

Introduction

My attitude formation started early. By the age of three, I was used to seeing my mother and father every day. The day after my father flew from Costa Rica to New York in 1963, I wanted to know where he was, even though I had been there to see him off the prior day. And I asked about him again the next day, and the next, until he became a memory kept alive only by my mother and her family with the promise that one day soon we would all be together again. "Soon" turned into 18 months. Our family, with the addition of my brother Carlos, born 3 months after my father departed, lived together in Amsterdam, New York until my mother experienced a bout of postpartum depression after the birth of my brother Roberto two years later. This event required all of us, except my father, to travel back to Costa Rica so my mother could get the constant help she needed. Again, I wanted to know when I would next see my father.

This time it was three years. Some of that time was spent without my mother as well, because she left us in the care of my grandparents in Costa Rica so she could reunite with her husband and begin anew. Eventually I joined my parents in the United States—this time in Lincolnton, North Carolina. Can you imagine how traumatic it was to sit in that fourth-grade classroom in Lincolnton, not knowing one word of English, and not seeing one person who resembled me, spoke like me, or even knew where I came from.

I was so happy to be reunited with my parents and my three brothers for Christmas in 1970. Carlos, Roberto and I had lived with my grandparents for almost three years, so we had never met our brother Mark, born in 1969. Our sister Martha came along in 1972. In my preteen years I didn't know the word *attitude*, but I did understand the isolation my family experienced by not having relatives nearby. Other than the friends we made at church, we were a group unto ourselves. But our parents kept us proud of our heritage.

I had heard the word *attitude* by the time I was a teenager, and I soon began to know the racist attitude some "good people" taught their children. I struggled then to understand why those kids behaved as they did, but it's clear to me today why my father changed his name from Gerardo to Jerry, and why my two youngest siblings don't have Hispanic names.

In 1971 I was the first Hispanic child to enter the Lincoln County school system. My father was the first management-level "foreigner" in the regional textile industry. He never spoke to me about the challenges he faced in an environment barely beginning to emerge from a history of segregation; but I knew otherwise. It was the tribulations and expectations of my parents, however, that helped me forge a deep level of pride about who we were and where we were going. What they taught us—their children—was the need for a positive attitude. Unfortunately, I didn't absorb much of the lesson until several years after my father passed away.

For the past 21 years I have worked through a series of mergers and acquisitions in the tumultuous banking industry. I've lived in four states and ten cities. My "M.O." is to take something that is failing and make it successful. The interesting and concurrent thread in these endeavors is that all of these turnarounds have been accomplished while working with mostly the same "struggling" participants who were there on my first day. I didn't realize until recently that the participants' attitudes, positive or negative, were also contagious.

I didn't plan to write this book. The president of our company, Kelly King, was making a presentation to my peer group of managers some years ago and stated, as he often does, that an individual's success depends on an Enthusiastic Positive Attitude, or EPA. I had used the phrase often in my "evangelical" speeches over the years, and had even quoted Mr. King in my Stonier Graduate School of Banking thesis on his theory of EPA. On this particular day, he made the comment personal by saying, "Positive attitude is a theme Luis should one day write a book about." This soft charge and my lifelong search to understand why things are as they are have led me to share with you what I consider to be the difference between failure and success; a happy and productive life or one filled with yearning and disappointment, personal fulfillment or the desperation of emptiness.

This book is not:

- A magic potion to make everything all right. Our lives will never be completely right.
- A multistep program leading to some dramatic change or understanding what aligns the stars and planets. Some people can change through these programs, but some lose heart when results are not what they think they ought to be.
- A treatise on Pollyanna attitudes focusing on feel-good behaviors. There are times when you'll feel bad and you should—until you change the outcome.

Because of the huge amount of input we receive from diverse sources every day, our attention spans are short, so this book is compact on purpose. It's digestible and focuses on an achievable theme. I hope you will benefit by spending a short amount of your valuable time in these pages.

—Luis Lobo

CHAPTER 1

Why?

Why do people fail?

Have you ever heard someone describing another person as "such a nice guy that I just don't understand why he can't make it happen." Or, "If so and so would only do 'this,' he/she would be so successful. He/she just simply will not listen!"

Being too nice or not listening is not the problem. I believe people fail for several tangible reasons. For one, they may have a sense of entitlement and believe, even after a series of setbacks, that success will be handed to them on a platter, silver or otherwise. These individuals are not grounded in reality. They may have also been given a false example of what it takes to be successful, and when they employ this method they fail because the template is unethical or not based on reality.

But primarily, I think people fail because of a fear of failing. You have heard this before, but let me qualify the phrase "fear of failure." People driven by this fear are so focused on doing everything possible to avoid a setback that they lose balance with their personal, familial and spiritual lives. I know this type of person well. I have seen him in the mirror for 40 years. Some people will tell you, "You have to have balance." The problem is that they can't tell you how to obtain balance, and more than likely, they have their own struggles with the scales of life.

Success is an ongoing series of steps toward a desired goal that, in time, allows us to look back and gain confidence for future steps. I often tell team members who are anxious about off-target results, "If the past has been a glorious path, why would the future be any different?" This is something I also have to self-coach on when my anxiety builds around some less-than-desirable result or new challenge.

Gaining confidence from prior positive experiences, however

small, coupled with the steps and behaviors necessary to attain the desired outcome, will ease your fear of failure, but it never completely goes away. Once your confidence improves, you may start to define the fear as a feeling that helps focus you to do a good job. Yet, not understanding how this emotional response to a nonexistent danger comes about can lead to a life filled with dread and workaholic characteristics. Sure, this emotion may provide you with professional success and opulence, but these often come at the cost of failed marriages, distant familial relations, and an unresolved understanding of yourself. In other words, have faith in the steps you are taking and make sure you continue to take them.

Another way fear of failure manifests itself is by keeping us on our conventional route and not letting us take new paths. This paralysis is responsible for a lack of action and keeps many people from attaining a higher level of success. This condition also resonates with the too-familiar "He/she chose not to change and is now out of a job, a marriage, etc."

The simplest way to move away from this choke-hold is to begin imitating successful people. What do successful people do consistently? Find out and then do those same things over and over again. Not to become that person, but to make those behaviors part of your own personality. This approach fosters a healthy attitude as the results begin to improve.

I have often heard that it takes 30 days to become accustomed to a new process and at least 60 days to dismantle an old habit (good or bad). I am amazed at how diligent I have been with my daily exercise regimen (6:30 in the morning!) and what a struggle it still is to manage my weight. You see, I have made a habit of exercising, but I haven't come to terms with the fact that my metabolism has slowed as I have aged. Therefore, it continues to be a struggle. The truth is that I have accepted the need for exercise to counter the reality of aging, but I continue to be bothered by the imbalance. This will not change until I face the issue head-on and begin a process. It's up to me.

Since we are creatures of habit, making changes is hard. If the issue we're facing is significant enough, such as giving up smoking after a heart attack, nothing less than a massive change plan is required, as taught by Anthony Robbins at his seminars. Robbins describes a profound new way of addressing things that need to be changed. But you can't go easily into his massive change plan. You have to plunge into cold water by stepping off the ledge, cold turkey. Just do it and stop talking about doing it! Enough already!

People, of course, fail for a myriad of other reasons as well. But it's OK to fail in the attempt to improve. Failing creates an enduring sense of confidence. President Theodore Roosevelt said it best in a speech before the Hamilton Club in Chicago on April 10, 1899:

Far better it is to dare mighty things, to win glorious triumphs, even though checkered by failure, than to take rank with those poor spirits who neither enjoy much nor suffer much, because they live in the gray twilight that knows not victory or defeat.... It is not the critic who counts, not the man who points out how the strong man stumbled or where the doer of deeds could have done them better. The credit belongs to the man who is actually in the arena; whose face is marred by dust and sweat and blood; who strives valiantly; who errs and comes short again and again; who knows the great enthusiasms, the great devotions, and spends himself in a worthy cause; who, at the best, knows in the end the triumph of high achievement; and who, at worst, if he fails, at least fails while daring greatly, so that his place shall never be with those cold and timid souls who know neither victory nor defeat.

Most often, we create the greatest barriers for our own good. This leads me to my next question: ***Why do most people underperform?***

I often hear folks talking about regrets. "If only this and that had happened, I could have been or done this and that." This is also known as the blame game. Some people learn to live with life's disappointments by blaming some force out of their control that keeps them from attaining their goals or aspirations. I believe most people underperform because they have placed the responsibility for their future and success on someone else's shoulders—an individual, an institution, a circumstance.

These people are unwilling, or perhaps not conscious enough, to seek the next step in their professional, personal or spiritual development. Even when opportunities are placed before them—maybe disguised as a career move to another city or state, maybe as a chance to help a needy family in their community—they will resist moving out of their comfort zones. In time, the offers cease to occur, and then they wonder why they never progressed, even though they were such dedicated employees, spouses or parishioners.

Most people underperform because they have not been given a proper template or a clear and consistent example of what can be accomplished. Even when role models are available, people have to be engaged and stretched through goals by "push-the-envelope" type leaders and teachers. If people are taught down to the lowest intellectual component in their group, they will probably become bored and resist additional learning. If they are challenged and the subject matter requires mental or physical effort, they will likely respond with enthusiasm and commitment.

When I was young, someone asked what my professional goal was, and I answered that it was to become a bank president. I planned then to keep reaching toward higher levels of achievement that would hopefully culminate in the actual goal. I say "hopefully" because I realized even then that we are able to mostly control our own contribution to an organization, but we can't control all the inputs that affect our goals.

It was through this awareness that I later began to redefine my professional goals. Today, my goal is to fully extract all the potential I have been given in whatever role I play and for all those I may represent. This is an outcome I can own. I have also applied this new definition to my personal, familial and spiritual lives. I believe that, with this definition, I will have greater ownership in my development and be able to move down life's paths without many regrets. This definition gives the responsibility for my future to me and away from those outside my control. It may be true that we control very little in life, but by influencing what we can, we move away from the feeling that our outcomes are in someone else's hands.

Why are 75% of people unhappy?

This is not a scientific finding proven through focus and control groups giving specific responses to specific questions. It just seems to me that one out of every four people I meet has a pretty good grasp on his or her purpose. The other three endure some ongoing issue with their work, family or spirituality. No, I don't associate with a large group of problematic and depressed folks. And, yes, I do recognize that all of us are not perpetually happy and fully focused 24/7. But assume for a moment that my observation coincides with your own view of society. How does the attitude of the 25% differ from that of the 75%?

Here I have to go back to Kelly King's theory of Enthusiastic Positive Attitude (EPA). Mr. King explained EPA in his 1981 banking thesis for the American Bankers Association Stonier Graduate School of Banking:

> *Given that attitudes can be measured, and with proper training can be changed, the question becomes: What attitude should bankers have to result in the best performance? Positive thinking philosophers, such as Dr. Norman Vincent Peale, have been saying for years that there is power in positive thinking. Other philosophies encourage enthusiasm as a way to be successful. Substantial evaluation results in the conclusion that an Enthusiastic Positive Attitude is the desired attitude for bankers in the 1980s. The value of such an*

attitude is so important that bankers will need to develop pro-grams to change attitudes in this direction.

This doesn't imply that we should never feel bad about some life event, occurrence or thought. Indeed, we are supposed to have negative feelings when we experience such issues. It is in the ongoing daily interactions with others and ourselves that negativity is manifest. A discourteous driver may anger us to such an extent that our entire day and all our human interchanges are ruined. Was this event significant enough to be allowed to waste our precious time? Maybe we have a sick relative or a significant life cycle issue such as the death of a loved one or a divorce. Is the response equal to the event?

Should these events cause us to drop off our calm precipice into anxiety and depression for years and even lifetimes? For some people, the grief or trauma is so deep and unrelenting that they can properly evaluate the situation and begin a journey back to life only through professional help. For many others, the response to these events goes unresolved, causing major and possibly irreparable damage to their hopes and aspirations. Cognitive dissonance occurs when people are aware that they must change their behaviors, but they are unwilling to change their beliefs.

When I see the symptoms of anxiety and depression in others, I try to guide them to a professional. Most people on emotional roller coasters don't seek assistance by themselves and are not guided by someone experienced in recognizing the signs, so they medicate their imbalance with drinking, smoking, spousal abuse, overeating, drugs, gambling, etc. Then they ride the vicious cycle downward.

You can't achieve EPA with a clinically unresolved matter in hand. And the treatment is much more effective when the patient knows that healing is possible and is positive and hopeful about working toward it. The American Psychiatric Association estimates that 20% of the population, more women than men, will experience a major depression in their lifetime. The other 80% may not go into an abyss, but a large percentage go on and off the roller coaster because they can't gain perspective on the situation—it's the vicious cycle I just described.

How can we put events into perspective?

I find it helpful to measure events by asking the following questions:

> • *Is the event life-threatening? In reality, 95% of situations don't fall into this category and shouldn't receive a full-blown fight or flee response.*

> • *Is the event important to my life goals? Some things are, but most are not, even though some situations, such as rudeness from someone we encounter at work or profanity in the media, may tend to truly aggravate us. If the event is important to our life goals, a response is necessary, but only to the extent that helps us add perspective.*

> • *Is the event within my sphere of influence or control? Most issues, such as trying to change another person's beliefs or our happiness or disgust with a political party or elected official, are not within our control and, at most, can only be slightly influenced. We may be able to offer another perspective that can help our friends gain greater dimension to their beliefs, and we can exercise our right to vote and thus try to influence the outcome of an election, but beyond that, we are very limited in our ability to influence or control anything.*

I am not advocating a numb and nonemotional state of being. When we answer the question, "Is this relevant to who I am?", we are able to measure our response and emotional state and then launch our attitude. It has been my experience that the things we allow to negatively impact our attitudes are often petty and irrelevant to our goals.

Have you met folks who have had traumatic life events and still go about life in a positive and constructive fashion? These individuals have gained an understanding of the specific event and their relation to it. And, sometimes alone, sometimes with the help of others, they have moved forward. They haven't allowed the event to have a negative impact or damage their goals.

So, to recap:

• *Many people fail because they hold unrealistic beliefs about what will bring them happiness and about the amount of effort necessary to attain their goals.*

• *Most people underperform because they have not been given a proper template or an example of what can be accomplished.*

• *Many people are unhappy because they are experiencing cognitive dissonance from knowing what they should be doing to enhance their lives but being unwilling to do so.*

• *How we react to outside stimuli largely determines our attitudes, so we should have a clear understanding of what matters to us and what merely aggravates us. The world would be a happier place if we all had a process to measure our response to life's challenges. I just gave you mine; hope it helps!*

CHAPTER 2

Be Who You Are!

Now that we are aware of the cause and effect of events on our emotions and attitudes, we can begin to gain ownership of this critical component to our spiritual, familial and professional lives.

I am now compelled to ask, "Who is in charge of *your* life, *your* future, *your* impact on others?" The easy answer is YOU, of course. President Lyndon Johnson, when questioned about his leadership in what would be known as the Great Society, said, "Doing the right thing is easy. It is knowing what the right thing to do is, that is hard."

We know who is in charge; what we don't know is what to *do*!

We are singular. There is not another human like us. Each of us is the genetic embodiment of millions of years of breeding. At birth, we begin to feel all our life experiences, both consciously and unconsciously.

Regardless of your religious beliefs about "original sin" or the theory that we are imperfect until we gain acceptance from some cultural or mystical essence, it is hard to dispute that a newborn child is as close to perfection as he or she will ever be. Granted, this new being has no understanding of the world and has not developed a set of values by which to reason and make decisions. The child has also not yet developed judgmental and discriminatory beliefs about others or self. This child has not yet experienced defeat, despair, fear or anxiety. It is through the examples seen and heard from primary caregivers, and those actually experienced, that the baby begins to develop a set of beliefs.

Some of these beliefs are based on reality and are easily integrated into our everyday lives, such as our belief in the freedoms granted by the Constitution and our espousal of a democratic society.

Other beliefs are *not* based on reality, and when exercised, they cause friction and a lack of integration within our self and our society. An example of this is the belief that a member of another race is more or less motivated or more or less intelligent than our own race. Exercising such beliefs prejudges others without allowing us to understand the individuals. It causes a division in our minds about how different we are from them, causing further isolation from one another. This isolation, in turn, causes us to remove these individuals from the pool from which we select friends, teachers, employees, and civic and religious organization members. By doing so, we harm our fellow humans by shattering their self-esteem, and we harm ourselves by excluding that person's potential to grow and contribute to our society and our own lives.

We have also developed a set of beliefs about ourselves—some based on reality and some based on emotional responses detached from reality. I clearly understand that I will never become a professional soccer player, even though I have enjoyed soccer from my earliest memory. But I have limited athletic ability and I'm a bit too old to sprint up and down the field. The fact that I lacked the higher skill required to reach this level of performance, and my unwillingness to train incessantly to achieve the necessary skills, formed the realization that I will never play professional soccer. Therefore, I do not have a shattering sense of failure about it.

However, I *have* had to overcome a sense of inadequacy seeded long ago by feedback that I was not good enough overall. When you have never played a school sport, you feel foolish trying to fit in with schoolmates who already have an understanding of the game. Add mockery, schoolyard teasing and insults to the mix and the result is either a child who quickly improves through natural ability and fits in, or one who retreats and avoids the pressure. I decided to retreat. The shame was that I discovered my ability for speed on the high-school track team, and later, after intense practice on the soccer field, I developed a feel for the soccer ball. But it was too late. Not having someone around who noticed my latent fire and offered guidance resulted in my avoiding the competitive athletic arena. What I did not realize was that this experience, coupled with the veiled discrimination I experienced in my teen years from peers, created a "take-no-prisoners" mindset in my college years. I was being fueled by an emotion not based in reality. Powerful rocket fuel indeed!

I have never been a cold and calculating person. However, I have never waited long for an opportunity to manifest itself, and I created opportunities as I went along. The fuel that drove me to earn two undergraduate degrees, an MBA, an honors degree from a national banking school, and certificates in other post-graduate work was partially driven by the belief that I was not good enough.

The problem is that this kind of fuel burns up the pilot as it propels the rocket. I truly appreciate having this negative driver pointed out to me at a self-awareness workshop, but it has taken several years, as well as much self-redevelopment, to replace the negative driver with a positive sense of being. I have also realized that we do not unlearn negative states of being. Instead, we become aware that they exist and then self-coach toward productive behavior. I am no less demanding of my personal or professional development than I was before. The difference is that now I do believe I am good enough to have a place at the table and feel confident in my ability to contribute to whatever forum I am involved in.

The possible result of never having identified the not-good-enough-driver would have been anxiety about my own competency—not only as a professional, but also as a father, a husband and all the other roles I play. Such a condition may have manifested itself in unproductive work relationships and, in time, stymied my career progression. It may have resulted in clinical anxiety, depression, ulcers and poor health. It may have eventually ruined not only my career but also my marriage and my faith in all I hold dear. The point is that, when I picked up this negative belief, it was fully based on emotions I felt. The reasons for my feelings were not based in reality, but they were certainly powerful. Always be aware of what is driving you.

I will also tell you that I have placed faith in many people along the way. I had to. But it is the *singular* individual responsibility one takes that makes the difference. As Kelly King says, "If it's to be, it's up to me." That says it all!

I mentioned earlier that we really control very little in life. Just imagine if we could control 50% of the input that goes into our behavioral equation! What would the result be? For example, we can't control all the inputs that assail our children, but if we can guide some of what they *do* receive, can it make a difference? What if the child, early on, recognizes love as it is shown to him or her by others and thus learns to live in a supportive environment? Does this learning have an effect when the child encounters an environment of tension and untrustworthiness? Of course! If he or she had encountered a *negative* environment first, negativity would be the template for how the world behaves, and the child would also tend to behave negatively. But by encountering a positive environment first, the child knows there is another way and can strive to change a negative environment if he or she wants to do so.

What if a team member has worked in an environment where errors were severely criticized and his or her opinion was rarely, if ever, sought? How will he or she behave when a new, enlightened manager arrives and asks for an opinion on something? The team member has been trained not to think, not to offer suggestions. The person's creativity has either been chastised directly or he or she has seen some other poor soul called on the carpet. This person is not willing to make mistakes, so he or she won't even be willing to *try* a new process, much less *suggest* one. The new leadership will fill the employee with anxiety and he or she may not hang around long enough to see the development of a holistic and positive work environment where people's opinions are respected, sought and implemented.

Why are folks surprised when the individual quits before the game starts? It's simple: the employee did not have a model of how things should be, and no one took the time when the new manager arrived to explain the new rules of engagement. Telling people how things will be different at least gives them hope and communicates intention. The lack of communication establishes confusion, sometimes with disastrous, unpredictable consequences, all in trying to change things for the better!

I remember Gerald Schrum, principal of Lincolnton Senior High in Lincolnton, North Carolina. I played in the stage band and Mr. Schrum would blow the saxophone with us occasionally, so I got to know him in a relaxed environment. I sought his guidance one day when I was feeling different and distanced. I asked him, "How should I act to fit in?" His words have carried me for 25 years.

He said, "Luis, just keep being the enthusiastic and friendly person you already are. It will carry you far." On that day, Mr. Schrum gave me a template, an example of self-worth that not even my parents could have given me. He gave me confidence that it was all right to be who I was. He helped guide the input and provided a foundation on which to build. I am amazed how far a kind word can carry a person.

Are we telling the truth to our employees? Are we engaging ourselves with our followers? Is our message clear? Are we consistent in delivering and "living" our message? Are we connecting with others and helping to interpret their perceptions? This is not being meddlesome. This is being a leader—someone who can have a significant effect on another.

The interesting thing is that most of us aren't very good at telling people when they are doing *well* in their roles either. Why? Because, deep inside, we believe it's not proper to have a deeper relationship with those we are supposed to lead, help, guide and mentor—somehow it makes us ineffective. How many times have we heard, "My father/mother never told me he/she loved me, but that's the way men/women were raised back then." Guess what? They still are! Parents need to understand the impact a parent-child relationship can have and make a point to show love. This will change the cycle by giving children the proper template.

When we make a connection at a deeper level, we form bonds of trust upon which all potential may grow. When we do not, we dehumanize one another as chattel, and the results are proportionate.

Can we control even half of the input others receive? During work hours, we have access to others at least 33% of the day. Can we have a positive effect on one another during this time? If I spend my leisure hours feeding my mind positive data, will this have some consequence? If I spend my leisure hours involved in a negative environment—rumor mongering, backbiting, complaining, etc.—will this also have some consequence?

The answers are all yes. We own what we allow to filter into our minds. We also have responsibility for what we "feed" and filter into other minds. By controlling some of the input, we may make a significant contribution to both ourselves and others!

CHAPTER 3

Becoming the YOU You Are to Be

"Esse Quam Videri," North Carolina's state motto, means "To be rather than to seem."

You are who you are! This is a reality. You can't be anyone else, and to attempt to be someone else causes confusion over your purpose in life and what you stand for. Sometimes this behavior is described as being fake, not being your own person, or acting and not being.

I believe people who feel compelled to act like someone else are doing so to fit in with another person or group, therefore compromising their identities for the perceived approval of others. This personality phenomenon occurs most often during early adolescence and young adulthood, when the struggle for acceptance is the most intense. The tragedy is that it lingers with too many people beyond this stage, and at its worst, creates individuals who subsist on others for their opinions, acceptance, social behaviors and beliefs.

Discrimination is a behavior emulated to conform to a group. We know that discrimination is unethical and not grounded in reality. Yet many people continue to quietly accept this bloodless crime so they won't be criticized in their group or community. I have known people who use racially derisive language even as they admit that all of humankind is created equally and is equal before the law. For example, "Boys are better in math than girls. Children from the Far East are more intelligent than children from the West. Men are better at managing money. Blacks have poor work ethics."

How can this dichotomy exist? It exists because people have allowed themselves to conform to another's belief and behavior even when it is not their own. I call this state of being *consensual ignorance*—being consciously aware that a truth exists, yet being unwilling to seek it or acknowledge it when confronted with the truth. If I dispute the law of gravity, then someone thoroughly describes the principles of gravity to me and I still dispel it, I have chosen to become a consensual ignoramus!

If a person is raised in an environment where certain peoples' ideas are discounted because of how they worship, how they look, or how they speak, does the individual have to continue to support this type of behavior? Or does he or she have the responsibility to make up his or her own mind? Not to have your own opinion is to become a psychological slave to another, and possibly become bound to a nonreality-based philosophy or set of beliefs. Do we just shake our heads at these individuals and steer a wide path around them? Many people do so, and in the process, give up an opportunity to help people realize that they can have their own beliefs, not someone else's. You can't make people change, but sometimes just giving them a glimpse of another viewpoint can be a catalyst for greater awareness.

While reading the previous paragraphs, have you felt uncomfortable at some belief you quietly espouse, yet truly regard as not based on reality?

There are those whose lives are changed because of one quick dramatic event such as a near-fatal accident or a religious conversion. For most of us, however, our life-changing events are normal occurrences: your company is merged, your marriage partner wants a divorce, your children declare themselves not mainstream in their beliefs. When our world is shaken up, we are forced to test our beliefs and can't rely on conventional wisdom to help us.

I now understand how siblings can go years, and even lifetimes, without speaking to one another due to some arbitrary belief or behavior that caused a rift in their relationship. I now understand how a father or mother can lose touch with a child due to some event that tested his or her moral beliefs. I now know how team members can lose their way by embracing things as they *were* and not as they have become.

In most cases, one side chose not to hear the other side because of a set of beliefs they picked up along the way. Sometimes these beliefs were grounded in fear or ignorance, but the beliefs and the consequences were *very real*.

You are a mix of every positive and negative experience you've consciously and unconsciously had every day of your life. You can't change your memory and you can't change the past. But you *can* become aware of what is real and what is not.

Accept yourself as you are and make up your own mind! Recognize that which is real and don't be driven by irrational emotion. **Please heed this warning:** Be very aware of what brings out the negative in you. It could be like Archie Bunker (an archetypical bigot with preconceived ideas about everything and everybody) suddenly realizing what he has become!

After you have accepted yourself and your beliefs have become your own through the integration of value judgments, find the courage to act on them. I realize this is easier said than done, and some people require professional assistance to overcome dramatic events in their lives that weigh down their potential. You can't erase these events from your memory, but you don't need to carry them on your shoulders as evidence that you are flawed. You are not flawed! You simply had a negative experience, more likely as the victim than the perpetrator. Left untreated, the memory can rear its ugly head and undermine your interactions with others. Once it's recognized and accepted, you can manage the feelings you get when your button gets pushed and react in the proper manner.

I am not attempting to help you deal with a personality disorder. That's between you and your doctor. What I am proposing is that *only you* have the power to change the way you evaluate and react to events. *Only you* can set your attitude to open your mind and appreciate another point of view. Can you imagine everyone suddenly deciding that we have all the knowledge we will ever need just because some experts said so? Preposterous as it sounds, too many of us do just that as we go through our everyday lives, never making up our own minds or sharing our own concepts. The freedom to *be* is the freedom to *think*!

When you have chosen the freedom to think and to formulate your own precepts, concepts and value judgments, you have chosen to become part of a solution instead of a reaction. Being part of a solution requires maintaining a positive and open attitude. To react to issues through emotions grounded in nonreality-based beliefs is to carry a filter that can produce a negative, close-minded attitude.

Stay the course! We are all a work in progress. I don't believe anyone just "arrives." Nobel Prize winners admit they have much more to learn about their chosen discipline. Religious leaders state that their faith grows through a greater understanding of the power of love. Artists reflect their feelings through their work in an ever-expanding ripple. I like to describe our journey toward knowledge, competence and love as an onion we keep peeling, sans the aroma, until we arrive at the end of our days.

What all this means for goal setting.

Face it: The most important goals you will strive to attain are those you set, not the ones handed to you. This is your life, not a life at the disposal of another. What are your intellectual goals? Goals for your professional life? Goals toward your loved ones? What are your goals toward your faith?

See it first! Stephen Covey, the famous behavioral author, said we must "begin with the end in mind." In other words, "see" yourself at the next level or the next or the next—visualize crossing that imaginary milestone. And seek this vision often.

Now become very clear on what is required to reach this level. Don't attempt to figure it out by yourself; get feedback from others. Seek the advice of individuals who can give you perspective—people who are actively engaged in living and achieving. Seek advice from those no longer among the living as well! Read biographies and auto-biographies of individuals who attained a high level of contribution to their chosen fields. Stretch your mind by reading in areas where you have little knowledge or experience. Then you'll understand the historical perspective of how ideas were developed, how one event led to another, why things are as they are, and finally, how things can be influenced toward a better conclusion (or at least a better path).

There is no value in knowledge that is not used for the betterment of humanity. People who don't use their mental abilities as part of the solution to our world's challenges are at best intellectual hobbyists. I conduct leadership seminars at several colleges and universities, and one of my favorite postings on the chalkboard prior to my presentation says, "To avoid criticism: Say nothing, think nothing, be nothing."

The reality is that, when you think and act on your beliefs, you invite a reaction, sometimes positive and sometimes negative, and it is through these reactions that we create dialog and a clearer perspective.

Great leaders, great thinkers, great athletes, great everythings are not born, they are created through a ceaseless, persistent and indomitable desire to attain a higher level of contribution. Once on this road, you'll face many deterrents, but your determination and desire, once flamed, will hopefully be unquenchable. Love of knowledge, love of excellence, and love of self are strong narcotics, so remember to gauge your progress, balance this quest with your other responsibilities, and avoid overcorrection. Seek a *gradual* and *consistent* path toward your goal.

In time you'll see the path you left behind as you continue to visualize the potential ahead. Many people don't give themselves the time necessary to establish this foundation, but just like an exercise regimen, goal setting is always for the long run. There are no quick fixes.

Staying on your mission path is seldom easy. It helps to look out for others on the journey—people who seek what you seek, even if on a different subject. It is satisfying to encounter these people along the way and to engage with others who want something other than immediate gratification. You may also be dismayed at how few seekers you encounter. Why are there so few? Because most individuals have chosen to allow others to think for them, thereby inadvertently choosing to become victims of their environments.

You are different. You have chosen to be the *master* of your destiny, or at least to have a significant influence on what happens to you, your family, your goals and your future. Have faith, stay the course! Attitude can change dark into light, fear into courage, mediocrity into excellence. It is your *attitude* that will keep you on task, your *attitude* that will help you get up from the stumbles, your *attitude* that will get you where you want to go. Not someone else. YOU!

CHAPTER 4:
An All-the-Time Job!

Vacations should be wonderful opportunities to get a little closer to our loved ones, to learn about a new subject or geographic area, and to simply rest and relax. I'm sorry to tell you that there is no vacation on your quest for greater awareness, greater competence and greater understanding. There is no time out for irrelevance, no postponement of growth potential, no going back. You are on... entirely.

I will warn you, however, that the road ahead will be complicated by many turns and detours. You must constantly ask yourself, "What am I seeking?" The answer will keep you true to your quest. Otherwise, you can become quickly enamored of, and just as suddenly disillusioned with, issue-reactive philosophies that stray you from your course.

Americans recently experienced a financial boom in technology markets, with lightning-quick changes in marketing, capitalization schemes and client perceptions. In the Internet marketplace, it became an accepted belief that earnings were secondary only to market share and first-to-market imperative, even if only with a concept, so as to gain capitalization and add users. The business plan could wait. This was the "new" economy and the "old" economic principles no longer applied. The stock price valuations of these "new" organizations dwarfed many large and consistently profitable corporations. Investors bid up the stock price to levels beyond the capacity of future earnings to sustain the present valuation. We were witnessing a surreal play on the world financial stage, and the actors were not only the companies involved, but also Joe and Mary down the street who could not pass up the opportunity to gain 20-50% on any firm with "dot com" at the end of its name. Then suddenly, when the next sucker chose not to step up, this pyramid of cards collapsed. Financial devastation eclipsed many dot coms, their employees were laid off, and stock portfolios were decimated across the spectrum of otherwise cautious investors.

This is a long way of telling you that there will always be a diversity of ideas challenging the status quo. This is how we progress. When you decide to earnestly support or bandwagon a cause or faction, choose through your own induction and deduction. Don't be influenced to choose through the hype of media, the siren song of some guru with the new best seller, or your friends' raving. The sin of complicity is worse than the sin of omission. Inevitably, we may feel foolish for not becoming involved in some "new truth." Likewise, we will feel justified when it is proven that there never was any truth in the matter.

What are you seeking? Is the idea or theme compatible with the scope of your life quest? If not, it simply becomes noise and must be avoided. By using these filter questions, you can activate proper planning, execution and follow-through every day, almost every waking hour.

If I am determined to fully use every bit of my potential in my professional life, I am naturally going to contribute more than the average fellow. I'm going to integrate greater knowledge into my chosen subject because I am actively searching for new answers to the challenges at hand. I am going to think outside the box as I search for these new answers through information from diverse and remotely-linked sources. I will become an expert in my field because I have an all-consuming need to know more, to do more, to gain better results. It's a formula: Plan to gain knowledge, use the knowledge and results to gain more knowledge, and combine the results for better execution. Again and again. I call this **ambition**.

If I am driven to maximize my potential as a father, husband, brother and person, I am going to be engaged with the individuals in these relationships. Not *some* of the time, *all* of the time. I am not talking about simply being with someone all day, every day. I am referring to being a part of their life; being an active and caring resource that person can count as his or her own. I will seek to know this person, to learn their strengths and recognize their weaknesses, to know their dreams, and to assist them in personal development. I call this **love**, and I will attain it by using the same formula set out in the last paragraph.

If I am dedicated to fully developing my spiritual being, I am going to live the beliefs I hold. I can't just read scripture or go through some weekly ceremony. I must take the message and make it real in the world I inhabit. I must be the voice and the arms of the message. The impact I have on every human I encounter, and on those I will touch only through my actions in my professional and family life, is a manifestation of my spiritual self. I call this **faith**. It is also love and ambition, and I will attain it by using the same formula.

The three areas above—ambition, love and faith—are not either/or choices. They are each a complement to the others. When they are treated as either/or, we lose the way to happiness and fulfillment.

Your ambition, your love and your faith are all products of your attitude! A positive attitude will seek an environment where your professional goals are nurtured and realized with the cooperation of others. A positive attitude will allow you to understand the idiosyncrasies of others and respect their viewpoints even when in direct conflict with your own. A positive attitude will help you see the sameness in every individual.

Your newfound freedom to engage with others, to seek new sources of knowledge, and to respect other viewpoints are the fruits of a positive attitude. Now anything is possible. Before, you were limited by the walls of intolerance you built around your beliefs. Now you are free to seek the next level of competence in your field, in your personal life and in your spiritual self. Conservatives will see you as liberal, liberals will see you as disciplined. You will see the face of potential!

You will be amazed at the amount of new knowledge you are able to absorb in one sitting now—learning that would once have taken longer because of your lack of interest. Your personal life will be richer as you seek to understand before being understood (an important tenet of the famous prayer of St. Francis of Assisi and, according to Stephen Covey, one of the most important habits of successful people). The faith of your fathers now requires new mantles because of your greater understanding and awareness. Don't be surprised if others now see you as happier, less prone to temper tantrums, or more reflective.

It IS your attitude that is making all this progress possible and you are in control of this magnificent quality! CONGRATULATIONS!!!!

Can you give this gift to others? You can certainly try, but sometimes you can attempt to give other people a wondrous quality and their cynicism will keep them from realizing their good fortune. What you have attained is not easily transported into the belief template of another individual. It can be taught, but it must also be earned in the process so that it becomes the filter by which they view their world. Otherwise, people will revert to the negative filters that damage their potential.

Let's calculate the impact of a positive attitude as it is shared, or not, with at least one person on a given day:

Sally, Scenario One:

The manager doesn't have any experience in sensing Sally's feelings or, worse, doesn't feel it is important to get involved. Sally's behavior becomes morose, the quality of her work suffers, and she is reprimanded and eventually dismissed. The strain from the loss of her income and the emotional tension with her children and husband become intolerable. Sally is thrown into relentless anxiety, can't sleep and falls into despair. One day she decides it's all too much and takes her own life.

Sally, Scenario Two:

Sally has recently lost her mother to cancer and her home life has been deeply affected by the pain of her mother's illness and death. Sally is often given to bouts of melancholy, feels distanced from her husband, and at best, tolerates her three children. Her manager at work senses the distress Sally is enduring and asks to meet with her and discuss her feelings. This enlightened manager recognizes the symptoms of depression and refers Sally to the programs available to employees. Sally appreciates the concern and begins to participate in a program that proves helpful in realizing her abundant potential with her family, friends and work colleagues. Sally begins to improve mentally and her family and work environments brighten up.

Was the manager's disinterest a pivotal behavior in the outcomes just described? Can enthusiasm on a manager's part in helping to guide people to professional assistance make a difference? Maybe it's safer not to get involved, but at what cost? Are we our brother's keeper? I believe we are. We are given opportunities throughout our lives, much like the one described above, where a kind word, a helpful demeanor or a gentle suggestion made all the difference.

We could go further and calculate the ripple effect in a company, a church or a school, but I know you get the picture.

Jose Andres Arce Fernandez
My beloved maternal grandfather

Felicia Gonzales Herrera (forefront)
Maternal grandmother with my Mother as a baby held by a friend,
her sister Cecilia, my great-grandmother Domitila and
my great-great-grandmother Filomena.

My parents Marta and Gerardo Lobo
on their wedding day in 1959.

My father Luis Gerardo "Jerry" Lobo Avila

The author at 2 years old.
Enjoying the company of his grandfather

Coming to America at 5 years of age, September, 1965.

From center, my daughter Felicia, Debbie, Thomas,
Andres and Luis. At the posthumous awards ceremony
for Lifetime Achievement in honor of my father
— Diamante Awards

Luis G. Lobo is chosen by MBE Magazine
*as one of the 50 most influential minorities
in the U.S. in business, 2004.*

CHAPTER 5:
Be Reason Able!

Napoleon said, "God fights on the side of the army with the largest regiment." This is not meant in a disrespectful manner toward people's faith or as an argument about whether our prayers are answered. My grandfather often said, "God helps those who help themselves." The issue is: What can I do to get effective results, given that my attitude is in the right place?

REASONING!

John Allison, our Chairman of the Board at BB&T, explains reasoning as our learned ability to use deduction and induction with concepts and precepts based on reality. John explains reality as "what is, is." You can't change it, you can't make it up. It simply is.

My friend said, "If only I had purchased that insurance policy before Dad got sick, we wouldn't be in this financial condition." His situation was the consequence of an action not taken. The insurance policy was *not* purchased and his hardship became a reality. However, he learned that insurance is important to protect family and business interests. Not acting on this situation becomes a detachment from reality. When we're detached from reality, we often make decisions that conflict with a desired outcome. My friend's desired outcome is to protect his family and business interests from an untimely demise.

I don't profess to have even a sophomoric understanding of philosophy. But reading books on how to "think," particularly those on the discipline of objectivism, has given me a different perspective on how our emotions can drive us to make erroneous decisions. Emotions are very real and are most intense concerning issues or events that bring on fear or grief, or that clash with beliefs instilled in our psyche when we were young.

Fear is a primal reaction to the fight-or-flight response embedded in our DNA. We become more alert, adrenaline flows through our bloodstream, and we tense up and become aroused to visible and invisible (sometimes imagined) forces. Fear constrains our thinking process, so when we act out of fear, we often end up with an erroneous response.

Unrelenting fear can lead to anxiety and depression. The terrorist attacks of September 11, 2001 in New York, DC and Pennsylvania caused psychological damage even to people unrelated to the victims of these acts. Our blanket of security was pulled away and we all felt at risk. Our perspective of reality—being the masters of our destiny—was turned upside down in a matter of hours, and the new reality drenched us with a sense of foreboding. There have been volumes of analysis compiled on the political, economic and psychological precedents that may have led to the terrorist attacks. We all asked ourselves what we did as a community, a nation and a superpower to bring on these attacks with such ferocity. 9/11 affected every conscious citizen in the United States, as well as many others around the globe. We have been told to respond by continuing to live "normal" lives, spend money, and move forward. These instructions are an attempt to separate us from the world as it really is and make us believe that we can just wish away our fear and danger.

Living in the new reality and trying to behave as we did in the old reality is why, within 90 days of those horrible events, we were told by psychologists that many people disconnected to the tragedy (those who didn't lose loved ones) could not shake off the psychological trauma. The anxiety continued to manifest itself through sleepless nights, recurrent nightmares and a feeling of impending doom. It is interesting how we can't take the advice and separate the emotions at the same time.

I believe that, before we can accept what happened on 9/11, we must have a clear understanding of the world we face. We have to essentially rewrite our mental hard drives before we can begin to live our lives again. It's impossible to begin anew with the reality of yesterday, because that reality has changed. If people don't make this change in understanding, their emotional response will be negative.

We encounter these disconnects from a new reality even in the face of less significant changes. In my professional environment, I see this happen when a new merger is announced and the team members of the acquired institution try to change their understandings and beliefs to fit the corporate culture of the acquiring institution. Most do so and move on to new and rewarding careers, but some are unwilling to accept the fact that their professional environment has changed. This discontent is reflected in their attitudes and sometimes there is very little the organization can do to help these folks see the new opportunities available to them.

Every person who makes a change of this type has feelings of fear, uncertainty and instability in the process, but these emotions usually subside as his or her understanding and confidence increases. Many times, the difference between those people who make it and those who don't lies in the attitude of the individual—their willingness or unwillingness to give the changes a chance. Those who try to understand the new reality are, in essence, rewriting their hard drives as they experience their new environments, and they gain confidence through increased perspective. In time, we absorb a new or clarified set of beliefs that are consistent with the reality of the environment we inhabit. When the beliefs and the reality are consistent, we act in a manner conducive to our desired results.

I am not professionally competent to address the psychological response to grief either. I do know what deep-seated grief feels like, however, because I experienced it as a young adult with the passing of my maternal grandfather, Andres Arce, and again in my mid-thirties with the death of my father, Gerardo "Jerry" Lobo. In both instances, I was coached to give myself time, and both times I experienced severe feelings of loneliness and abandonment, even when surrounded by the families of four siblings, my own wife and children, and my relatives. I recall that, in both cases, I relieved my pain with the memories of the love these two men had unconditionally given their families. I remember trying to understand the role I should play in the void they left behind, knowing that their positive approach to life required the same of me. Twenty-five years after the passing of my grandfather, and ten years after the death of my father, I still think of them every day. There are times when the pain is very sharp at the thoughts of what might have been if they had survived to see the lives my brothers and I have crafted through their teachings. It is their memory, and the fact that we have progressed in ways that would be pleasing to them, that help me bear the grief. I have found fulfillment in the process of passing on their beliefs to my children; in this manner, their lives still matter.

This story reiterates the long-term effects of a positive attitude in the face of personal loss that barely abates with time. Many people rely on their faith, as I did, to help them deal with the confusion and pain associated with the passing of a loved one. I believe faith fortifies our attitudes and we gain greater understanding of how fleeting our lives can be. I also believe that we must devote every waking moment to the highest calling of our potential—personally, professionally and spiritually.

People experience myriad emotions when confronted with a statement or behavior that is contradictory to the beliefs we picked up early in life. I remember seeing an African-American for the first time when I was four. My feeling was one of novelty. I had not been embedded with any sort of negative belief about African-Americans. I also recall my confusion when, several years later, a primary school teacher admonished me for wearing the hat of an African-American boy by telling me I might "catch something." Why didn't she say that when I was wearing a white boy's hat? The law of contradiction says that something can *not* be and also *be* at the same time. This was my first experience with that law.

One of my relatives has a deep fear that people of a certain race are going to do him harm. He was taught this concept as a child to keep him away from members of that group. When this relative has more than casual conversation with members of this "harmful" race, he often comments about the nice person he just encountered. The group appears "abnormal," but the individuals seem very "normal." The individual encounters don't validate his beliefs about the group, yet the beliefs ingrained early on have only slightly dissolved.

I can clearly understand why there is distrust and hatred when members of different races are kept segregated as we were in the United States prior to the 1970s. Members of each race have the belief, handed down, generation to generation, that other races are a threat to their ways of life, or are less intelligent, or are superior, or are morally decadent, etc. When individuals of separate races begin to talk, it is amazing how much they appreciate the sameness in one another.

President John Kennedy, in a speech at American University in 1963, spoke about our common interests:

> *And if we can't end now our differences, at least we can help make the world safe for diversity. For, in the final analysis, our most basic common link is that we all inhabit this small planet. We all breathe the same air. We all cherish our children's future. And we are all mortal.*

If the truth is so evident and irrefutable, why do we as a society continue to harbor such ill will against those who look, act, pray or think differently from us? Because our beliefs are being tested. If we are willing to examine our beliefs and why we have them, we can begin to understand why we respond in a certain manner when our beliefs are challenged. This understanding can help us to lead more productive and responsible lives, and in the process, give our children a set of values based on reason, love and faith.

The operative word here is *reason*. To have and use reason requires our understanding of why things are as they are and what they should be. When we gain this perspective, we begin to change our beliefs and these new beliefs become consistent with the reality we face. Only then do our actions become congruent with our environment and we can begin to see positive results.

CHAPTER 6:
Have Faith!

In the New Testament Gospel according to Matthew (31-32), faith is proactive:

The kingdom of heaven is like a mustard seed that a person **took** *and* **sowed** *in the field. It is the smallest of all seeds, yet when full-grown, it is the largest of plants. It becomes a large bush, and the birds of the sky come and dwell in its branches.*

Does faith impact our attitudes?

Much like the mustard seed, faith in a greater power—spiritual or secular—as well as in ourselves, must be taken and sowed continuously. I am not speaking now of confidence. Confidence is how we feel by being well prepared to meet a specific challenge or how we feel in the discharge of duties after we're qualified and experienced. Faith is intangible. It is like a vapor, known yet unseen. Faith is given to others as it was to my siblings and me by my parents and grandparents. Faith is also what we have in others we trust because we know their character. Faith is not static. It grows within us, it's a *living faith* nurtured by our life experiences and how we embrace our everyday interactions. Adversity will challenge our faith, and as it does, it strengthens our faith.

How do we gain faith? Do we need to become part of an organized religion to find faith? Is there truly only one path to a fulfilled spiritual life? I like Thomas Jefferson's explanation of his faith in a letter to Ezra Stiles dated June 25, 1819, just a few years before his death at the age of 82.

In that branch of religion which regards the morality of life and the duties of a social being, which teaches us to love our neighbors as ourselves and to do good to all men, I am sure that you and I do not differ. We probably differ on that which relates to the dogmas of theology, the foundation of all sectarianism, and on which no two sects dream alike; for if they did, they would then be the same. You say you are a Calvinist. I am not. I am of a sect by myself, as far as I know.

I believe Jefferson concluded that a person's faith is his own and individuals have the right to worship or not worship as they see fit. This is evidenced in Jefferson's masterpiece, the Declaration of Independence, which put forth his belief in a creator that bestows "unalienable rights of life, liberty and pursuit of happiness." The liberty to hold our own beliefs is central to the success we have enjoyed as a nation. The great nation-states of antiquity, and even some in the modern era, have witnessed their undoing in part by forcing adherence to a state-sponsored religion or cult and codes that segregate according to religious preference. History gives us example after example of the butchering or extermination of people in the name of someone's god. We still have these forces within our own country, yet our novel concept of separation of church and state has nurtured tolerance and helped create a vast and rich diversity.

Each individual, with his or her own perspective, must answer the aforementioned questions of religious beliefs. I will only address the issue of how we can gain faith. Unlike trust, which can erode due to circumstances and which plays out between individuals and groups, faith is anchored by a deep-seated belief in a religious or secular power, or an idea, or a philosophy.

A faith based on religious tenets may include a moral code of how to behave, as well as full adherence to the religion's central entity. If we follow the instructions and give ourselves over to the entity, we are assured that our life is just. We gain faith through these beliefs.

Ultimately, faith in a secular institution can result in the domination of the follower, causing people to give up their independence to think and act. I am reminded here of ideologies like Socialism, Nazism, Communism and Fascism, which concentrate power in the state at the expense of the individual's freedom. Our own institutions (companies, not-for-profit organizations, governments, etc.), though certainly not the equivalent of those *isms*, are usually a reflection of their leadership and values, and that reflection can be positive *or* negative. When negative, our faith may be misplaced or abused.

Faith based on an idea is more precarious, because the idea must withstand challenges. Americans have faith that, through effort and diligence, they can acquire the skills and economic opportunity to better their station in life because all men are created equal. We have no caste systems to keep people from attaining their potential. This belief, although not applied to slaves or women when introduced in our Declaration of Independence, has been tested for over 200 years, and it's resulted in remarkable success by many people overcoming their beginnings.

Faith based on a philosophy is also precarious. Communism was a philosophy of egalitarianism. Property rights did not exist and the state controlled everything in the name of the "people." It was (and still is in Cuba) the prescribed philosophy by which to even out the economic imbalance between the haves and the have-nots. I believe communism failed because it took away the freedom of individuals to have faith in themselves by denying them the rewards of their efforts.

The philosophy of objectivism is one of clarity in the reality of the moment—take the facts as they are and make the best decision based on them. Only the facts matter. If you have all the facts, you can make the best decision. The pure implementation of this philosophy has its challenges, however, because it's opposed to any public support of people less fortunate than the median. Righting the wrong is left to the individual, not the government, thereby not imposing any additional burden on society. It took governmental action, such as the Civil

Rights Act of 1964, to force compliance with the belief that all people are created equal and should have access to equal education, housing and employment. In a perfect and just society, these issues would be moot. The problem is that we live in an imperfect world.

A person with a positive attitude has faith that his or her actions, based on his or her own beliefs, will gain the desired outcome. A lack of faith creates uncertainty, anxiety and lack of purpose. Goal-oriented individuals have a deep sense of faith in something or someone. They are driven by a conviction that the purpose and outcome of their lives are beneficial and justified. The greater this faith, the greater the person's commitment. I am reminded of the interminable experiments of Thomas Edison toward the invention of the light bulb. Nothing deterred him from his mission. It was said of Abraham Lincoln that he had failed so many times in his personal and professional life that gaining the White House seemed like a mirage in the desert—unreal and unattainable. These men had faith, at least in themselves.

I have the faith inspired in me by my parents and grandparents, although I did little with it for the first 15 years after my graduation from college. Sure, I had plenty of drive and ambition, but the drivers were negative in nature. I wanted only to show those who had excluded me, impress people with my accomplishments, exhibit my worth through my professional position. It was during a personal crisis several years after my father's death that I reached into the recesses of my heart and renewed my faith. During and after this two-year period (these things seldom happen overnight), I learned that most events in my life were outside my control. I learned that "I" must influence those events that I can, but with those I can't, I must have faith that the outcome will be all right. Sometimes the outcome is acceptable and sometimes it isn't. When it isn't, I ask myself what I could have done differently. In some cases, there are indeed things I could have changed, and from these I try to learn. There are also times when everything was prepared to the minutest detail and the outcome was not what I anticipated. It is not easy to accept a negative outcome, but if there isn't anything that could have been done to alter it, we have to move on. Faith is what helps us get up from our failures.

Webster's defines faith as: "1 (a) allegiance to duty or a person; loyalty; (b) fidelity to one's promises; 2 (a) belief and trust in, and loyalty to, God; (b) firm belief in something for which there is no proof."

I describe faith as belief in my purpose, grounded by an understanding that I do not travel alone. I am sustained by my faith, encouraged by it, centered by it. I have my own religious beliefs, of course, but this description is what faith *does* for me, not how I *relate* to it.

We gain faith by the conviction of our beliefs. Our faith also helps others develop faith by observing how we react to circumstances. My father encountered significant adversity in his personal and professional life, yet I never heard him complain that life was unjust. He was grounded in the conviction that his purpose was whole, that helping others was his calling, and that providing his children with the environment and education to use their minds was worthy and noble.

Because of my father's efforts, there is a growing and prosperous Hispanic community in Lincoln County, North Carolina. He was the first Hispanic there, and he opened the doors of economic prosperity for those who would make the most of it. Oddly, not all people *want* to walk through the door of prosperity, because of the responsibilities it carries. You can't just go to a house of worship and order up a serving of faith. It must be purchased with the coinage of sweat, trial and tribulation. Many of the Hispanics who followed my father to Lincolnton chose not to stay—some for family reasons and some because the change necessary to succeed was too traumatic. They chose familiarity because they didn't have faith, and returned to their homeland. Those with faith experienced dramatic changes.

A person of faith is undeterred by failure, by obstacles or by naysayers. These people understand that failure is a frequent companion to faith, and with each stumble they come nearer their goal. It is said that adversity is the mother of invention. This is true not because everyone reacts the same way to adversity, but because of their faith, some adjust in the process.

I am fortunate to have had a long and gratifying friendship with the Reverend Oscar Burnett, O.S.B., Abbot Emeritus of Belmont Abbey in Belmont, North Carolina. I met Father Oscar when I arrived at The Abbey as an 18-year-old freshman. He was then acting as head of campus ministry. He reached out to the freshmen and involved many of us in campus coffeehouse functions. His hearty laugh, caring demeanor and listening skills pulled many students through trying times. Father Oscar, and a few others, never wavered in their faith in me, and because of their interest, I have overcome quite a few daunting challenges. A simple, kind word may be all it takes to help someone gather the strength to move forward.

Have faith!

CHAPTER 7:

Keep it Simple.
Say it Often.
Make it Burn!

Having provided the financing for the renovations, I attended the rededication of a local Methodist church in Burlington, North Carolina several years ago. The bishop gave a sermon that has stayed with me ever since. His message was one of leadership through a positive attitude. His prescription was the following:

1. Keep it simple.
2. Say it often.
3. Make it burn!

I have come to realize that this formula works for the folks being led and for the ones leading. It even works when the *group* is doing the leading. Nido Qubein, renowned speaker and author and a member of BB&T's corporate board of directors, said, "You can't *think* your way into acting positively, but you can *act* your way into thinking positively."

The three steps outlined in this chapter can help you do this. How? My 11 year-old son Andres explained it in the following manner:

When you have an idea, you have to make it simple—not too simple, but simple. Explain it to your friends to the point they know what you are talking about. You need to constantly remind them of the idea. Remember, remind them like when your teachers did in middle school about some book report that's due at a certain time.

From the mouth of babes . . .
The Methodist bishop in Burlington was illustrating the following:

1. **Keep it Simple: Have clarity of purpose**. Why are we here? What is our purpose? Why do we do what we do?

2. **Say it Often: Repeat, repeat, repeat the purpose.** Harold Geneen, when he was Chairman of ITT, noted that if he wanted anything accomplished, he had to say it at least 100 times. Regardless of the week you attend mass in a Catholic Church, you will hear a repeat of the Gospel from the same time last year. The message seldom changes. It just becomes reinforced through the interpretation of the celebrant and our current events.

3. **Make it burn: Make it real for all involved.** In my professional world of sales leadership, habits don't become real until you make the salesperson accountable for a certain behavior and the results that should manifest through that behavior. Broadcasting the message is necessary so that everyone gets on the same sheet of music, but you can't be sure the behaviors are being implemented until you hold the individual accountable. Consistently.

Keep it simple. Clarity of purpose is crucial for individuals and organizations to be able to execute their stated purpose consistently. Recall the communication game where one person whispers something to the person seated next to him or her, then the receiver whispers what he or she heard to the next person and so on. By the time the last person announces to the group what he or she heard, it is usually quite different from the original message.

We know that disconnects have occurred when people hear the same message but come up with interpretations different from each other, and to some degree different from what the speaker meant to communicate. There is always the message you *intended* to communicate, there is what you *actually said*, and there is what the others *heard*. It's no wonder that marriages, partnerships, families and both formal and informal organizations fall apart because of poor communication.

How can the sender become more effective at crafting the message for greater understanding, effectiveness and implementation? My prescription is to *take out the fluff.* Focus on the main message and explain why you are saying this, doing this, asking for this. Then ask the audience for feedback on how the information may affect their situations. Sometimes the feedback occurs in the Q&A period after a presentation; sometimes it's face to face, over the telephone, on video, or through email. It is always best accomplished in a group setting however, as people often build understanding on a question or statement made by another. Some people, although they may not say anything, can be confused about some portion of the issue. Inviting them to call you or e-mail you afterwards helps these silent types gain understanding and feel included.

I am continuously in awe of the capacity of team members to execute very complicated processes but, at the same time, be blown away by failures in seemingly simple strategies. How is this possible? Because the messages for the more complicated processes are usually fully explained, make sense and are achievable. Simple strategies often occur because of the reverse: they were confusing and tough to achieve because they were not explained carefully, therefore not completely understood.

Here are a few simple ways to make your message clearer:

1. Explain why. I can't emphasize this enough! People usually resist change unless they understand its purpose. Even if the change makes sense to you, you better get buy in from them.
2. Don't read to your audience! They can read for themselves (they *should* be able to anyway). You may want to use a handout of major points along with a tool for illustration, such as PowerPoint slides or charts or boards. To be effective, you have to *engage* the audience, whether face-to-face, on the telephone, or in writing. The longer the message, the less likely it will be listened to—that's reality!

3. It is not necessary to have the delivery skills of a revival preacher or a master orator, but some level of enthusiasm by the speaker helps the audience get the message. You can learn to become a more effective speaker by watching great speakers.

4. Never take more than 15 minutes to explain your case, because at 20 minutes you have lost the audience (unless you have moved to a different topic). Finished or not, stop at 15 minutes and request permission to conclude. This break brings your audience back to the message.

5. Ask the audience for feedback, but be ready to prompt your own, in case you encounter the mute group.

Say it often. Aristotle is credited with saying that excellence is a habit formed. We form habits by repeating actions that we have gained acceptance for, whether in public or in private. Likewise, repeating your central theme or purpose over and over through different media helps people recognize the stability and endurance of your message. In time, they will act on it because it has become a part of their belief system.

I often refer to myself as a scratched record. (For you young folks, records were the ancestors of cassette tapes, which preceded CDs, which preceded DVDs.). When a record was scratched, it tended to repeat the same line over and over. I work hard at staying on message, repeating why and supporting appropriate behavior by reflecting it back to the central theme. Religions have gained continuity through this tactic. So can your message. You will appear well grounded and a source of strength for the group, for your family and for yourself.

Everything you do needs to support your purpose, and your message must always resonate to your purpose. Once you have a disconnect in your behavior and your message (do as I say and not as I do), you begin to breed confusion and discontent, not only in your group but also within yourself.

Stay on message and you will gather followers!

Make it burn. Talking about your purpose or message or point is necessary for common understanding. Explaining it over and over is necessary for clarity and focus. But it will never become real until you make it real for each individual involved. This requires your personal participation and dealing with the results. If the results are appropriate, it's because the individuals are gaining in understanding and gradually improving. If the results are not appropriate, avoidance by the leader, parent or coach will only make it worse.

By making your purpose or message or point burn, you make it real and accountable, and you involve the ego of the individuals. When a person's ego is affected by feedback given or by the outcome of results, a positive effect will occur in his or her attitude. In the beginning it may seem that you have caused fear, resentment and even hostility between you and your team or family member. Some people have such brittle egos that they will seek to protect their feelings by running away, resigning, moving out of the house, avoiding others, or any number of other negative coping actions. The more resilient ones will grow through the process instead, and their attitudes will move to higher planes through your factual and timely feedback.

You can help others have a positive attitude, but in most cases they need to go through a personal or professional growth experience to gain the perspective required to form a better one. When people are progressing through change, you should stay in close contact with them, yet not be overbearing, so they understand that you are trying to help them improve, not persecuting them. I often tell my teammates that if I wanted them to fail, I would just let them be and allow them to cause their own demise. By involving myself, I am giving of my time and experience to help them succeed. When you involve yourself with your team members, positive possibilities abound. When you ignore or lose contact with your team members, you plant the seeds of their failure…and your own.

Leadership is never a popularity contest and effective leaders are seldom those who give in to groupthink (the tendency of group members to conform rather than to think independently or critically, first described by Irving L. Janis) or the isolated opinions of "those in the know." People will give you a thousand reasons why they can't accomplish what you are requesting. They will point out every obstacle, real or imagined, that keeps them from the goal. They will begin to convince one another that the goal is unattainable (groupthink), and overall performance will begin to diminish. Then a negative attitude will envelop everyone on the team as their emotions spiral downward. This is what happens in the absence of leadership.

In the presence of leadership, the leader is focused and convinced that the goal can be attained, and he or she gives example after example of "ordinary people doing extraordinary things." The leader exposes the reasons people are blaming obstacles for their failures and dissects the "untrue beliefs" that are causing negative thinking. The leader proactively deals with the purveyors of negativity in leadership positions, giving them the option of leading to the goal or leaving the group in quick order. The leader coaches the players on what it takes to attain the goal, helps create "heroes" who go for the goal, and rewards even the slightest behavior toward the goal. When others see that the goal can be attained, even in places "different" from other areas where the goal is being met, they will begin to work toward the goal too. Those who don't proactively participate can't be part of the team.

This is how you make it burn. Someday I want to cross paths with that Methodist bishop again and thank him for the simple process that has helped others and me over the years. Funny how even faith has to be nurtured along!

CHAPTER 8:

YOU Matter!

My son Andres and I often take Sunday walks around the high-school track close to our home. The topic of discussion is sometimes "the meaning of life," and over the last couple of years, we have peeled this onion, layer by layer. I have concluded that all meaning in the life we lead is most significantly produced by ourselves. In other words, the individual is the one who gives meaning to his or her life, not circumstances before, during or at the end of his or her existence. It is mostly up to the individuals how meaningfully their lives are invested in the 70+ years allocated to them. I understand that many are born into poverty, disability, abuse and prejudice. But most of us in the U.S.A. are born into average circumstances.

Your future is up to you and only you. This is a disappointing discovery to those who want to blame every defeat, even before they begin the race, on some circumstance, person or organization. It is easier to blame than to try.

I have reached another conclusion: Be careful what you ask for! On a Tuesday morning, I began my new assignment as Regional President of the Potomac Region of BB&T in Frederick, Maryland. Remember in the wonderful movie, *The Wizard of Oz*, when Dorothy runs into her house as the tornado nears and jumps on her bed as the house is picked up by the storm? Suddenly the house falls back to earth, and when she opens the door, everything is in color! Dorothy says to her dog, "Toto, I don't think we're in Kansas anymore." On that day, I realized I was not in my version of Kansas anymore either.

Three weeks earlier, my boss, Chris Henson, came into my office and told me I had been promoted to regional president. He continued to speak for a few minutes, but I don't recall much of what he said. Into my mind came images of my father—a 21-year-old man landing at

Kennedy International in New York with nothing more than an address and $50 cash in his pocket. My mind filled with images of my parents toiling in textile mills to provide the means to educate their children in a foreign land. I remembered my maternal grandfather telling me in his letters how to behave and to have faith and to dedicate myself to learning. Then I thought of my mother, who was visiting Costa Rica at the time, and my wife Debbie and our children.

My first telephone call was to Debbie. When I told her I had attained my professional goal, she said that I had worked hard and deserved it. My next call was to my mother. I thanked her for all the sacrifices she, my father and my family endured to give us a chance.

Not only would we be moving our family again, with all the challenges involved, but I would now encounter a 184-year-old organization that was 11 months out of conversion to the BB&T systems and processes. To add something to the challenge, a group of former employees decided to begin a new bank about 90 days after conversion, calling on our client base as their primary targets.

I would have to call on all of my skills of assimilation, professional experience and human and financial acumen. I also needed a strong personal belief that the task at hand was doable. But I knew my *attitude* would be the deciding factor of how well our team would perform. It is always the leadership, good or bad, that determines the outcome.

It was quickly evident to me that all 300 team members wanted to do the right thing, but they were confused about what the right thing was. This was reflected in the utilization of systems, processes, leadership, teamwork, everything. It was also evident to me that these were bright folks who were proud of their work.

I told them I believed that not only could we create a high-performing region within the BB&T system, but we could create the highest-performing regional bank in the world! Now, Mr. Lobo, walk the talk...again!

Some examples come to mind of what great leaders have done in times of tribulation: Winston Churchill holding together the spirit of

Britain during the months of German bombardment before the U.S. entered the war; Edmond G. Ross, U.S. senator from Kansas, going against the pressure from his own party to cast the deciding vote on the impeachment of President Andrew Johnson—Ross knowing that, by doing so, our system of government would prevail and also knowing that his alienation was certain from then on; the Reverend Martin Luther King leading the cause for civil rights under ever-present humiliation and threats of death.

My personal example of leadership in difficult times may not have required the courage of the individuals noted above, but it has required focus, tenacity and daily human connectivity. First I had to communicate our purpose to the team. Each of our eight business line managers had to center the minds of their team members on the value they provide to our clients as trusted financial advisors, even if they didn't yet see themselves this way. Our purpose had to be explained as bringing hope and positive outcomes to our clients' financial condition and creating self-actualization for each of our team members in the process. This doesn't occur because we each *say* it. It begins when we make it real by modeling it, by inspecting the interactions between team members and clients, and by rewarding the big *and* small interactions.

The first order of business before my arrival was to call the members of the senior leadership team (SLT) to say hello. My first week in Frederick was spent meeting with each member of our SLT to learn about them, their roles and how they saw our future. Most of the time, I received a message of hope and bright expectations. The rest of the people were concerned about the challenges, confusion and frustration from clients and bankers. I acknowledged each experience as real, and with the input of two SLT members I had known in prior roles, sought to integrate the divergent pieces in my mind.

The early conclusion was that there had been some challenges with the conversion 11 months before, but most of these issues had been resolved. What had not been resolved was the negative perception many retail and commercial clients still had about the bank and the direction the region would take. So the question was: how can we begin to change the perceptions of our internal and external clients? I believe clients view the bank through the eyes of our team members. If our team members are dedicated to providing warm, proactive service to our clients, our clients will have a positive regard for the bank, even in the face of system mistakes and team members "learning" the process. Clients become dissatisfied when they encounter disinterested service and "blame-it-on-the-system" attitudes.

With this understanding of reality as we knew it, we spent our first SLT meeting crafting behaviors and goals that would address the negative perceptions. We crafted the following steps:

1. Communicate our mission to our team members at every turn and to our clients verbally and visually in our bank lobbies.
2. Begin our client contact process by setting the number and type of client contacts each of our bankers would make. This process would be launched immediately and inspected weekly.
3. Convene an officer meeting within 30 days to share our regional goals for the remainder of the year.
4. Provide each of our bankers with a personalized action plan by which his or her behaviors and results would be measured at mid-year and at the end of the year.
5. Facilitate a method by which we could have consistent contact with other members of the SLT and at least one monthly coaching session with me.

None of these actions were original to our bank; they were established processes within the BB&T system. They were, however, new to this group, and rarely do groups or individuals react positively to change, even when the change is logically viewed as constructive.

What ensued was the perception of "working harder" than ever before. I heard that my new nickname was "Luis Lots-of-Work." The reality was that we were just learning new processes, which always causes destabilization as people begin to cast off old methods and adopt new ones. I recall one member of our group walking around with 20 file folders under her arm just to keep up with the changes.

I have often been criticized for being quick on the trigger, yet I have never apologized for doing what is required *now*. I have learned that soft-pedaling gets you there later and prolongs the agony of change.

In the first month, I had occasion to visit with several of my former bosses at group meetings or on the telephone. I sought their advice on how to proceed and what behaviors or processes they were employing that gained win-win results. My former manager, Vince Nelson, who has known me the longest, told me to do what I had always done before, therefore reaffirming that giving direction and energizing the team would continue to work. My first manager at BB&T, Steve Wiggs, shared how he was scheduled to visit clients with his commercial bankers twice a week and reserved at least one hour a month for each of his direct reports for their needs. This is the same person who taught me to execute as close to the model as possible, which causes the greatest amount of discomfort but yields the best and fastest results. My most recent manager, Chris Henson, had shown me that consistently touching our team members forges team cohesion and connects our mission to our clients. One early coach, Rob Greene, again shared his message of 13 years prior: "If you are doing the right thing, the right things will follow," which I interpreted as being ethically focused and never wavering from our purpose. Allen White, the bank's sales manager and one of the fairest individuals I have ever met, told me how my leadership behaviors would positively impact the region, "seeing" into the future and giving me a visualization of hope. My present manager, Mike Oster, predicted a "best team" execution for our Maryland franchise.

I am grateful to each of these men for giving me perspective and sharing their best practices, which we were able to overlay on our region as we strived to gain momentum in the early months of my leadership. A good coach will never lie to you, but if you don't put his or her recommendations into action, you are the one deceiving yourself and your team.

Despite the fact that the Potomac team had undergone all the training provided to a new team, and in some cases were provided retraining of specific roles and processes, we had leaders perplexed as to why better results in client satisfaction and sales were not forthcoming. The answer is that all the training in the world will not change behaviors. Only involved leadership can change behaviors, and then your organization changes. You can't lead from the rear. If you do, you will become disengaged from reality and your team won't know its purpose. Leadership must be engaged, just as we require our bankers to proactively engage their clients without an obvious request. Leaders must be involved in the professional lives of their followers. My belief in daily interaction with the SLT members brought a great amount of satisfaction to some, and a career evaluation to others.

It may be that having our first officer meeting at the end of the day caught everyone fatigued, but I couldn't gather any group excitement from the audience. The next day I dissected the message, my tone, the hour of the meeting. Why had the meeting seemed flat? I finally realized that words would not energize this group. Only *action* from me and members of the SLT would begin to fuel their engines.

In March, I began my Tuesday/Thursday calling schedule with our commercial bankers to visit their clients and assure them that we were striving for their financial well-being. I had another revelation during these meetings too: their satisfaction was with the *banker*, not with the *bank*. When there was dissatisfaction, it seemed to occur because the client was disconnected with the banker and did not perceive an advocate within the organization. It then became easy to blame the bank, since many people don't want to direct their dissatisfaction toward an individual. Another revelation was that these clients were pretty happy, which was in contrast to what I was being told by several members of the SLT. Why the disconnect?

We were fortunate to have one business line that was beginning to really catch its stride: our team of young business bankers who focus their energy on what we define as Small Business. The interesting fact here is that most of the team was made up of recent hires from other organizations. I like to say that people can be successful just because they don't know it can't be done. I am not sure if this applies to anyone on this team, but it was apparent that they didn't have any "baggage" about the past or the changes. They had encountered change, and caused change, by leaving their organizations and making a conscious decision to join our bank. We had our first $1,000,000 lender on this team in March, and recreated the "Howlin' Wolf Award" (*Lobo* means *Wolf* in Spanish). We began to actively discuss what this team was doing to gain such significant results. We had some of the team members talk about their behavior on sales calls, and we wrote call reports to be circulated around the region for everyone to read. At the end of the first quarter, I bestowed the "Coach of the Quarter Award" to their leader, Rick Scheller. We were beginning to see what success looked like in our organization.

Another team was also beginning to reflect significant improvement: our service team of tellers and area-operations managers. This is our largest group, consisting of 120 tellers, led in seven clusters by their managers. The conundrum here was how was this group so proactive in client service, notably in teller referrals, and in reducing turnover in the teller ranks month after month? I decided to go into the branches unannounced over a two-day period and observe and ask questions. To my surprise, the tellers were full of optimism. My question was, "What is your area-operations manager doing to help you succeed?" The unequivocal answer was, "He/she spends time with me." Some knew to call this behavior *coaching*, others just knew their manager was interested in them. In my interviews with several area-operations managers, they described the scheduled coaching and tools they were using to connect with their tellers. The line manager, Jeff Margeson, had embraced the coaching model when it was presented at one of his meetings, and he implemented the process methodically. It was for this reason that Jeff received the "Coach of the Quarter Award" for the second quarter.

My questions were outpacing the answers! Why did these two teams have such significant results? Other teams were struggling to succeed with the very same client base, but why?

My role for the past seven years had been as the retail banking manager in two different regions. Our retail bank manager in the Potomac Region received a host of processes that had been proven in my former regions and other regions, but I am not sure anyone had ever encountered the amount of change during my first 90 days that his team of financial center managers did. To their credit, they were already gaining momentum in lending volumes, and when we introduced a temporary, attractively priced, structured loan product, their numbers went over the bank average. In April, we had two "Howlin' Wolf Award" members from this group.

Now the internal pressure to perform had become intense. There was a gulf of disparity between performing teams and non-performing teams.

The next team to catch fire was our mortgage lending group. It was led by a positive thinker who worked diligently to establish contact between his bankers and the community. Everyone can look like a hero during peak refinancing periods, but Alan Vendouern kept his eye on what happens when the rates normalize and we have to earn our business through purchases. His leadership has also spilled into the opportunity that exists among his bankers, retail bankers who help consolidate checking accounts and credit cards, and commercial bankers who create connections to builders and developers. His leadership has engaged his bankers internally and externally, and for that he was awarded the "Coach of the Quarter Award" in the SLT for the third quarter.

We were seeing this rapid evolution of success from several teams, but there was still a feeling that people in our community were not happy with the bank.

I felt compelled to find a way to transfer the positive feeling of our clients to our bankers in general—in essence, to overwrite their own negative perceptions of the bank. In my prior role in Virginia, we had periodically scheduled a regionwide calling night; our bankers called our best retail clients to tell them how much we appreciated their business and to ask for suggestions on how we could improve. We normally did this in the spring and early fall. This would be my first experience calling retail clients in this area. I was asked to call clients in our oldest location, downtown Frederick. When I arrived that afternoon to make my calls, I was surprised to hear that the team had concluded their calls ahead of schedule. And they were astonished at how happy the clients were. Sure, some servicing items were brought up, but 95% of our clients were happy! Boy, did I gain courage to make my calls!

Within the first two minutes of my conversations, each client made sure to tell me how "Suzie" did a great job, or that "Mary" and the team at "XYZ" branch were wonderful. I thanked each for the opportunity to be of service to their families, and said we hoped they would recommend us to their friends.

I believe we are wired to connect with one another, but we develop coping mechanisms to "protect" us from one another. These cause our demise by creating unnecessary divisions that lead to significant social problems. The least of these is rude behavior, the worst is racism. But I believe there is a "sameness" to us all, and people will positively react to the true unselfish humanity we each possess.

The call nights not only reconnected us with our clients, they helped our team members realize the value they add to our community. A similar event involving our commercial clients garnered the same satisfied results several months later. If negativity existed, it existed mainly in our own minds.

I was preparing to schedule the mid-year reviews of the SLT when

I received the resignation of two line managers. Both had decided to pursue careers at other institutions for different reasons. The first emotion from some members of the organization was fear. Something must be wrong with us and our region if members of the SLT are resigning. We acknowledged their departure and openly affirmed that we needed their contribution, but we maintained our focus on clients and, in short order, brought in replacements. The most amazing dynamic occurred within 60 days of these resignations: their teams moved quickly to the next level and never looked back, much to the surprise of many!

We believe we can continue to improve as we learn more about our clients, and can create not only the best regional bank in the world, but an environment that espouses innovation in developing the tools we need to maintain our competitive advantage. I believe we, the team members and our clients, are the competitive advantage—not our products, not even our brands. Upon my arrival in Frederick our regional team was ranked nearly dead last. As this book goes to press and in little over two years our team is now ranked in the top nine of BB&T's 38 regional teams.

So, do YOU matter? The power of YOU is yet unknown. I am not referring to you the reader, but to you the human being. Can people move mountains simply through the depth of their commitment to excellence? Yes! Commitment causes your mind to devise ways to move the mountain.

Because of one person, YOU, in concert with others through the ages, we have gained sufficient knowledge to extend the productivity of our lives. One hundred years ago, a 40-year-old man or woman was considered old. Today, many of us can't envision retirement; we gain too much self-worth by being productive. My grandmother Felicia chides people who comment on the "good old days." She remembers the early 20th century as a time of physical exhaustion and social seclusion. She considers her breakaway from the farm to an accounting career with my grandfather to be the springboard for their children's future. Have we gained an advantage in being able to use our minds as opposed to our backs?

Many are concerned that our country will arrive at a point where we "make" nothing and solely produce "services." If so, the world will probably continue to beat a path to our front door for technological advances gained in the pursuit of knowledge. These advances will be aided by technology, but the ideas will be birthed by us—YOU!

Do YOU matter . . . if you aren't the leader of your department, not the leader of your community group, not the head of a family? If you are 18 or 80, considered too young to know much or too old to adapt? If you don't have a formal education? If you have been raised to believe that one person can't make a difference? Yes! History is full of individuals who, through their single-minded doggedness, made significant contributions to their society. What distinguished each of them from the rest of their society was their belief that they mattered.

YOU **do** matter!

My accountant grandfather used to say, "To make money, a man needs capital." I agree that to take advantage of the opportunities that come to us almost daily we must be prepared to act. Wallflowers are rarely invited to the dance. When we are deciding who should lead a certain team in our bank or region, the choices are limited. If we chose by tenure, formal education or experience, we would have many candidates. We choose by performance, so the candidates are few. My message here is that you have the personal responsibility to make yourself matter. If you don't take on this commitment, no one else will take an interest in doing so on your behalf.

We are all hoping for the best. I have come to accept that you can't wish success unto others. They have to want it for themselves. YOU must be the driver on your life's path. Everyone can cheer you on, and others can provide you the resources for success. You can grow up in a loving and supportive environment. Every door of opportunity may be available to you. But if you're only a passenger on this trip, you will either fail or come up short of your potential.

My counsel to others has been of the here and now. Sure, they can decide that "this" is not for them and convince themselves that they are meant for another path. But what happens when they encounter adversity again? Do they keep conning themselves that "this" too was not meant for them while their future continues on a wandering path? Or will they stand and make their best effort there and then? Some of these decisions have immediate results and others are played out over the long run. It would be sad to look back 20 years from now and realize that they had the capacity and the ability to have attained their goals but never followed through. Regrets are possibly the heaviest baggage we can carry.

Hope with action (which is different from a reaction to environmental stimulus) equals results, and YOU matter in the outcome. There are outcomes every day, every year, for every lifetime. Placing the responsibility for your outcomes on another person, institution or circumstance is like regressing to the helplessness of a child. In many cases, the person who does this self-victimizes almost to the state of slavery—being told what to do, when to do it, and where to show up. Sadly, many people do behave this way today. The "contractual" agreement between the worker and the company has dramatically changed since the 1970s, but our psyches have not. Many people still think they are owed something because they have shown up for the last 5-30 years. Then they go into shock when their firm sells or fails. Although there are many guiltless victims in these situations, many allowed others to decide their financial and human potential outcomes. They victimized themselves.

I will not accept victims in our organization. I want only involved participants who are trying to learn more every day to achieve a benefit for their clients, their team members, and their organization. I believe we, each of us, YOU, have your hands on the controls that will largely determine your outcome. Recall Chapter 2 detailing "inputs." When you seek the inputs, the outcomes are more reliable.

I challenge my students at the BB&T Banking School at Wake Forest University in Winston-Salem, North Carolina, and those at the

American Bankers Association Stonier Graduate School of Banking at Georgetown University in Washington, DC, to gain a foothold of influence in their organization through their contribution. We are all seeking better ideas. Higher levels of management don't have all the answers to the challenges that face us today and will face us tomorrow. YOU do matter, and you must make yourself matter more by trying new and different approaches, gaining deeper insight, challenging the "given reality," and creating a better mousetrap. Waiting your turn for a promotion will only cause you to feel unworthy. Waiting for someone to notice you because you showed up every day will cause you to wait interminably and feel betrayed. Waiting for happiness to arrive will cause you disappointment. These things are bestowed on those who seek them. They are not handed out, they are earned. These ideas are not the stuff of genius, just that extra effort that garners a better solution. Then, and only then, will you differentiate yourself and gain a listening and seeing audience.

Just about everything in our lives can be proactively or reactively influenced by us to some degree. I may not be able to control the deforestation of the Amazon basin, but I can become a fierce advocate for conservation and teach people who will teach others the value of our forests. I may not be able to stop ethnic cleansing, but I can teach respect for others and live a life of mutual understanding with those outside my racial and philosophical groups. I may not be able to alter some people's perception that capitalism is fueled by greed and self-interest, but I can help create economic progress in the open market by helping my clients attain their financial goals through proactive planning and advice.

Our planet has become a small, interconnected village. I recall an interview my father gave in the early 1980s about whether the political problems rampant in Nicaragua and El Salvador could affect the sovereignty of our beloved Costa Rica. He considered these problems as being in our own back yard, even though Vietnam's problems a decade earlier had been on the other side of the globe. The reality is that the other side of the globe is now our own back yard.

Our freedom to *think* has become a real and present threat to many people, and their only response is violence against the innocent. These individuals, as savagely as they act and as noble as they perceive their cause to be, actually believe they can make a difference. There is nothing more dangerous to the status quo than individuals who are clear on their purpose and willing to die for a cause. These people have motives far different from those of the people who are trying to improve the global condition. The motivation is to influence. The outcomes are polar opposites.

This is not meant as a political discussion, only a reflection of the need for involvement and the poor dividends of detachment. We, as a free society, if we ever thought we could live our lives without a thought of those outside our borders, have been abruptly awakened. The paradigm now is that YOU do matter, both singularly and collectively.

CHAPTER 9:

What Do I Do Now?

"It all sounds good, Luis," I hope you're thinking. "So how do I start?" The following are the top ten behaviors that, over time, can give you a more positive attitude as you travel down this one-way street called Life:

1. Regardless of your beginnings, coach yourself that you are worthy of happiness and success in whatever environment you choose to exist in.

2. Don't believe you are "good at this" and "not good at that." These are untrue beliefs. You are capable of learning whatever you set your mind to master. What comes easy, we tend to label "good." What is difficult, we tend to label "not good." The reality is that if we dedicate ourselves to any task, we can improve. Never give up!

3. Move away from the blanket of familiarity and the Linus complex. (The "Peanuts" comic strip character Linus never went anywhere or felt confident enough to do anything when not in possession of his favorite blanket.) To understand others and gain a healthier perspective, you must cross paths with those who think, live and act differently. Immerse your children in mixed environments and you will give them coping skills superior to most.

4. Read, read, read! My seventh-grade language-arts teacher told us she didn't care if we read pornography as long as we read something! This statement flew over my head because I didn't know the meaning of the word, but I did understand the value of learning by watching my grandparents and aunts devour books of diverse themes. To this day I feel most comfortable surrounded by books. I encourage you to read the following books and papers: *The Seekers, The Creators,* and *The Discoverers* by Daniel J. Boorstin

The Visit by Friedrich Durrenmatt

OBJECTIVISM: The Philosophy of Ayn Rand by Leonard Peikoff

The Grand Inquisitor from The Brothers Karamazov by Fyodor Dostoevsky (web)

Undaunted Courage by Stephen Ambrose

President Kennedy and President Nixon by Richard Reeves

Letter from Birmingham City Jail by Martin Luther King (web)

The Closing of the Western Mind by Charles Freeman

The books of *Job* and *Ecclesiastes* in the Old Testament

5. Find a civic cause in your community and become active. JFK said most of our problems are manmade and so can be solved by good men and women. Become part of the solution. Remember that it is easy to criticize, but no one seeks out the critic. People seek out doers.

6. Become an expert at something in your professional life. Be the one who knows the most, talks the most, and involves others in a greater understanding of whatever your slice of expertise may be. Then you will connect more easily to areas previously foreign to you.

7. Be enthusiastic. The saying, "Nothing great was ever accomplished without enthusiasm" gives the essence of motivation. Enthusiasm is the expression of your motivation. It is also contagious, as evidenced by Tom Sawyer's teambuilding session of painting the fence. People will begin to see you as someone who has purpose, and they will want to be part of it.

8. Cleanse your palate often. Take off the blinders (originally placed on a horse's head so the horse could only see in front and would not be distracted by peripheral activity). Have multiple interests in your life. If you are a single person, have lots of interests—they will connect you with more people. Humans are communal and are not meant to live lonely lives. In time you will experience the relatedness of all things and begin to appreciate diversity as sameness.

9. Sweat profusely! Exercise and exertion have all kinds of physical and mental benefits. High performers need a stress buster that is healthy and beneficial—as opposed to alcohol, smoking and overeating.

10. Be kind to yourself. Accept yourself and be aware of your negative drivers. By doing so, you will be kinder to others; and people the world over respond favorably to a nice person. Good people don't necessarily finish last...or first. They simply have a better time at the race!

Good luck on your journey!

CHAPTER 10:

When the Dark Days Come and Linger, and They Will

Dark days are guaranteed to happen. I recall being 14 and thinking how wonderful it was to have my grandparents and great-grandparents alive. I even had the privilege of meeting my maternal great-great-grandmother, an event I still recall even though I was just four years old. Then, in rapid order, my great-grandparents passed away, followed by my maternal grandfather when I was a sophomore in college. My grandfather was my best friend during my childhood and teen years, he was the man who served as father when mine left us to come to the United States, and the man with whom I corresponded regularly after I left the nest. Grandfather Andres taught me how to play the guitar and gave me a moral code to live by. Without realizing the pain I was experiencing after his death, I immersed myself in my undergraduate studies, but I recall feeling abandoned for many years after his passing.

The most significant grief I have ever experienced occurred with the death of my father at the age of 52. I stood tall and honored my father at his funeral, as did my brothers and sister. We took good care of my mother and tried to move on with our lives. Then that sense of abandonment came back. Two years later, I began to have headaches. One of these was so painful that it woke me in the middle of the night. For two months, I slept just a few hours a night and could not understand the origin of the headaches. Neither could a host of doctors. Three months later, I had convinced myself that I had some terminal disease and began a precipitous downward emotional cycle. I finally found the right specialist, one who understood the symptoms of anxiety and depression, and over time, I made a full recovery.

During and after this experience, I tried to rationalize the origin of the illness: trying to do too many things and simply fatiguing myself, losing my faith in God and being punished for it, experiencing massive change (bank merger, job change, home purchase, death of father, reestablishing my professional persona). Others chimed in with their opinions: too focused on career, God taking you down a notch or two (not sure why), etc.

Looking back, my emotional and physical responses during this time seem like a bad dream. A cocktail of circumstances all arrived in close proximity and BAM, there I went. I had dealt with the past situations, but they had been buried in shallow graves. It was my father's passing that scratched off the scab and fully destabilized the belief set I had adopted many years before. My recovery was more intellectual than psychological. I "grew up" and began to fully assess my weaknesses and my gifts. I started to understand what was meaningful, what was trivial, and how fleeting time was. My life became my own, not my family's. My morals became my own as I embraced reality and cast off guilt and mystical beliefs. My faith became my own as I recognized God as without boundaries. I was still Luis, but now I was clearly on my path.

A loved one will be lost, your business may fail, you may lose your job, all your possessions may be burned, your marriage may dissolve, a crippling illness may limit your future. Some of these events will occur without notice, such as an accidental death or a house fire. Some will happen over time, such as a deteriorating marriage, a failing business, or declining health. You may have no interest or energy to even get up from your bed. You may feel that life is not worth living and there is not hope. You may feel abandoned by family and friends. These emotions are all perfectly normal responses. Somehow you must rationally convince yourself that "this too shall pass."

The only thing you can "own" during these traumatic events is *your attitude*. "What can I accomplish with the situation as it is?" is the only question that can give you a true answer. Dwelling on the past and licking the wounds can hardly be avoided, but you must push on in the situation as it is. Surrounding yourself with enthusiastic and caring individuals will help you deal with the trauma and gain a foothold on the future. Time is the only salve that can heal these deep fissures, and in some cases they will heal only superficially. A day does not pass that I don't miss my father. But I also don't let a day pass without telling and showing my children how much I love them. By doing so, I am preparing my children to be able to recall our full, unqualified relationship, not one filled with regrets.

Regardless of your situation, tomorrow will arrive, the sun will rise, and the world will move on. You must persuade yourself to move on too. You must drastically change your environment so your mind can focus on something other than your loss. By engaging yourself in proactive and productive endeavors, time will pass less encumbered by invasive thoughts of the negative event. Strong and consistent exercise can help you deal with anxiety and tire your body so you can find restful sleep. When medical assistance is necessary, it should be coupled with lots of activity and exercise. Rarely does medicine or therapy work well without these.

My grandfather told me that death is the circumstance we should have the least concern for, because it's guaranteed to occur. Ben Franklin said the same of taxes. We will all live out our lives, and all that we hold dear, materially and emotionally, will cease to exist. That is reality. Between now and then, we have the opportunity to live our lives as we see fit. Unfortunately, it seems like many people are waiting for something to happen to make their life better. Maybe this is why people, as a rule, don't like change. They would just as soon continue to endure a bad situation as it is because the change may be even harder. I have met people in miserable relationships who have no intention of changing their circumstances, haven't you? The devil you know is better than the one you don't.

But the positive societal changes of the last 100 years, such as insuring the rights of women and minorities, have been gained by seeking unfamiliarity—by change. None of these improvements have occurred without resistance, sometimes even by those who would benefit most from the changes. I have read about slaves not wanting to leave their plantations because that was the only life they knew. I have known women convulsed in fear because they needed to seek employment when their husbands walked out on them. I hear regularly about individuals not voting, even though many people have died to give them the right to do so.

We are all guaranteed some trauma in our lives. All of these situations require the active participation of the person affected to overcome the situation.

Our response, our *attitude*, to challenging experiences is the key to recovery and greater awareness.

FINAL WORDS.

It is my sincere wish that you have reflected on your own situation as you have read these few pages. We will live out our entire lives with ourselves. Sure, we will have friends and family but we are truly alone with ourselves our entire lives. Being honest with your "self" and living a life of crafted purpose can only be achieved with a positive attitude.

ABOUT THE AUTHOR
Luis G. Lobo

Mr. Lobo has been featured on National Public Radio's program "Marketplace" and in several national and regional publications. He was named by *Minority Business Entrepreneur* magazine as one of the "fifty most influential minorities in American business" in 2004.

Mr. Lobo is the Regional President for Branch Bank and Trust Company's (BB&T) Potomac Region based in Frederick, Maryland. He is also Chairman of BB&T's Hispanic Segment Task Force. BB&T is one of the largest banks in the United States.

Mr. Lobo is proud of his upbringing and education. He was born in Costa Rica and raised in western North Carolina in Lincoln County (west of Charlotte). He graduated from Belmont Abbey College in 1983 with a double major in economics and business administration. He earned an MBA from Campbell University and received a degree with honors from the American Bankers Association Stonier Graduate School of Banking at the University of Delaware in 1998. He graduated from the University of North Carolina—Chapel Hill in the Advanced Management Program in 1999.

Mr. Lobo is an active participant in his community. He is a Past President of the Southern Pines Jaycees near Pinehurst, N.C.; Past President of the Apex Chamber of Commerce, and the 35th President of the Apex Rotary Club near Raleigh. He was named Apex Citizen of the Year in 1993. More recently, he was President of the Professional Latin American Association in Norfolk. Mr. Lobo lectures extensively at colleges, universities and financial industry forums across the U.S. speaking on "Change Management," "Leadership," and "Sales Culture." Mr. Lobo is on the faculty of the BB&T Banking School at Wake Forest University and The American Bankers Association Stonier Graduate School of Banking at Georgetown University.

Mr. Lobo is married with three children.